Cordially yours,
Ethel Stephens Arnett

Books by Ethel Stephens Arnett

GREENSBORO, NORTH CAROLINA:
THE COUNTY SEAT OF GUILFORD
A history of the development of this progressive city

O. HENRY FROM POLECAT CREEK
An account of the first half of the short-story writer's life

WILLIAM SWAIM, FIGHTING EDITOR:
THE STORY OF O. HENRY'S GRANDFATHER
The record of a reformer, who inspired state progress

FROM ENGLAND TO NORTH CAROLINA,
TWO SPECIAL GIFTS
A tracing of England's illustrious Shirley family, which produced William Tryon and O. Henry.

CONFEDERATE GUNS WERE STACKED
AT GREENSBORO, NORTH CAROLINA
A report of the last days of the Civil War

MRS. JAMES MADISON:
THE INCOMPARABLE DOLLEY
A fully documented biography of the Nation's First Lady

FOR WHOM
OUR PUBLIC SCHOOLS WERE NAMED,
GREENSBORO, NORTH CAROLINA
Brief biographies of thirty-seven worthy persons for whom our public schools were named and sketches of ten historic places where the schools were named for the communities of their location.

THE SAURA AND KEYAUWEE
IN THE LAND THAT BECAME
GUILFORD, RANDOLPH, AND ROCKINGHAM
An account of the American Indians who were the first known inhabitants of the area.

Distributed by
Straughan's Book Shop, Inc.
Greensboro, North Carolina 27402

THE
SAURA AND KEYAUWEE
IN THE LAND THAT
BECAME GUILFORD,
RANDOLPH, AND
ROCKINGHAM

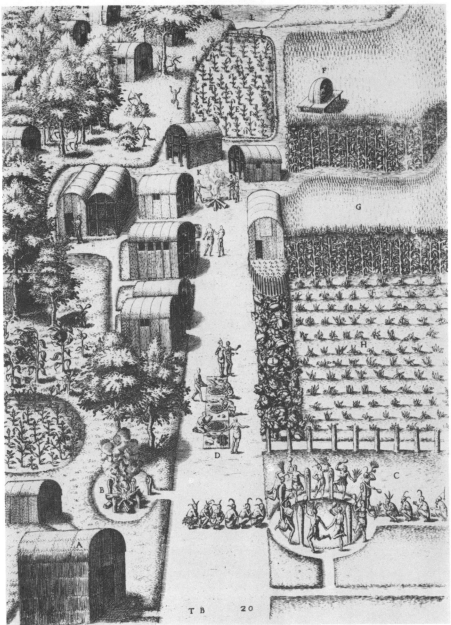

AN INDIAN VILLAGE

(A) A tomb of famous tribal ancestors. (B) A place where the Indians assembled and made their solemn prayers. (C) A broad plot where they met to celebrate their main feasts. (D) A spot where Indians made merry together. (E) A field of tobacco. (F) A field of corn with a guard house for a watchman whose continual loud cries frightened away large flocks of birds and herds of wild animals. (G) A field of corn choked to death because it was planted too close together. (H) A field of corn with broad furrows which produced the best yield.

THE
SAURA AND KEYAUWEE IN THE LAND THAT BECAME GUILFORD, RANDOLPH, AND ROCKINGHAM

ETHEL STEPHENS ARNETT

Smithsonian Institution, National Anthropological Archives

SIOUX INDIAN CHIEF

Media, Inc., Printers and Publishers
Greensboro, North Carolina
1975

This account of the Saura and Keyauwee Indians in the land that became Guilford, Randolph, and Rockingham Counties is published by the North Carolina Delta Kappa Gamma Society as a part of the American Revolution Bicentennial Celebration.

FOREWORD

Three men, who lived for a time among the American Indians in the land that became North Carolina, left the best accounts of the first inhabitants of this state.

First, John White, who came with the second group of Englishmen to set foot on present-day North Carolina (1585), painted from life pictures of Indians, which are copied in this book.

Second, John Lawson, who wrote the first *History of North Carolina*, actually traveled (1701) 1,000 miles and visited with tribe after tribe in order to learn Indian ways of life. He began his book with the statement that earlier English writers about America had been interested in the New World mostly as a trading center. He described such historians: "'Tis a great Misfortune that most of our Travelers, who go to this vast Continent in America, are Persons of the meaner Sort, and generally, of a very slender Education; who being hired by Merchants to trade amongst the Indians, in which Voyages they often spend several years, are yet, at their Return, uncapable of giving any reasonable Account of what they met withal in those remote Parts; . . . I have, in the following Sheets, given you a Faithful Account thereof; wherein I have laid down Everything with Impartiality and Truth." After eight years of association with the Indians, his book was published in 1709; and since then it has been considered the most authentic record on Indian life in North Carolina in the early 1700s. Lawson's history is especially important to this account, because he visited the Keyauwee tribe for several days.

Third, William Byrd, who is famous for his *History of the Dividing Line* (1728) between North Carolina and Virginia, is particularly valuable to this description because he furnished more information than any other writer on the Saura tribe.

VII

Although these men recorded their impressions in two different centuries, so strong was Indian adherence to their traditional dress and customs that John White's late sixteenth century drawings were similar to the Indian life and customs described by Lawson and Byrd in the early eighteenth century.

This account of the Saura and Keyauwee is based mainly on the records of these three men—on White for the illustrations and on Lawson for the story. Other accredited books on Indian life in North Carolina have been consulted and are listed on page 90.

For assistance in the preparation of this piece, I am deeply indebted to Dr. Joffre L. Coe, Professor of Anthropology, The University of North Carolina at Chapel Hill, who checked the manuscript for historical accuracy; to Josephine Hege, Associate Professor of History, Emeritus, The University of North Carolina at Greensboro, who edited the work; to Ann McKaughan Farrell, former owner and director of the Book Shop and former president of the Art Shop, in Greensboro, who made helpful suggestions from the viewpoint of the reader; to Eugenia Hunter and Dorothy McNairy, former presidents of the North Carolina Delta Kappa Gamma Society, who approved of the writing and plan of the work; to Matthew Hodgson, Director of the University of North Carolina Press, who granted permission for the use of John Lawson's *History of North Carolina* and John White's drawings as the main primary sources for the book; to the President and Fellows of Harvard College for granting permission to use *The Prose Works of William Byrd of Westover*, edited by Louis B. Wright, as another primary source; and to Virginia D. Powell, Director for 22 years of the Grimsley High Yearbook, who read both the galley and page proof of this book.

—Ethel Stephens Arnett

CONTENTS

ILLUSTRATIONS

* A Theodor de Bry engraving of a John White drawing.

I

WILD ANIMALS LED PEOPLE
INTO A NEW WORLD

The soil of Guilford, Randolph, and Rockingham Counties never lets us forget that it once belonged to the American Indians. In many sections of these North Carolina counties the earth is constantly giving up arrowheads, stone axes, beads, seashells, pieces of pottery, and crude farming tools as reminders of former Indian life. Called the "Red Men," they were the first people now known to have lived in this New World.

From what place did these first settlers come? According to John Lawson in his *History of North Carolina*, the Indians' answer to that question was, *"Where the sun sleeps our forefathers came thence."* It is now believed that between 20,000 and 30,000 years ago Indians began to follow the wild animals of Asia through northeastern Siberia, as they wandered by way of the Bering Strait into Alaska. This passageway was at times a broad stretch of land, estimated at 1300 miles across, over which men and beasts traveled in search of food.

These people, now known as Early Americans, depended mainly upon the use of animal products for their existence—animal meat furnished food and animal skins provided clothing and shelter. As great herds

1

of large mammoth, bison, buffalo, giant bear, and smaller prey roamed out of Alaska into Canada and down the river valleys east of the Rocky Mountains, the people followed. For thousands of years this gateway to the New World was open; and as the people multiplied they gradually scattered and eventually spread themselves all over North and South America.

Now that we know how the Indians came to this country, other questions arise: who were these people and why were they called Indians? Written records about them tell us that they belonged to the Mongoloid race. That means that they came from a racial stock that is native to northern and eastern Asia, which stock is distinguished as one of the major racial divisions of mankind. Detailed descriptions of the physical features of the Mongoloid race easily match those of the full-blooded Indian.

Why, then, were these people of Asian descent called Indians? The answer is simple. When Columbus discovered America in 1492, he thought he had found a new route to India, and from that belief the American natives thereafter were called Indians. For 483 years that mistaken name has remained unchanged.

The fact that Columbus was greeted by friendly natives does not necessarily mean that they were the first human beings ever to set foot on this soil. Lawson in his history called attention to the remains of much earlier inhabitants when "we found, in digging of a Well

2

that was twenty-six foot deep, at the Bottom thereof, many large Pieces of the Tulip-Tree, and several other sorts of Wood," which grew naturally only in the New World. Other items which were found in digging were pieces of "Earthern Pots," and they inspired thoughts of earlier wanderers who did not stay long periods at certain sites; they continued to travel with no particular place they could call home.

In the first half of the 1900s, serious investigation of early relics was undertaken in Piedmont North Carolina. In *Archeology of the Eastern United States* (1952), a chapter was included on: "The Cultural Sequence of the North Carolina Piedmont," by Joffre L. Coe, Director, Laboratory of Anthropology, University of North Carolina at Chapel Hill. Dr. Coe gave special thought to "The Guilford Focus," which was descriptive of the Piedmont area. "All known Guilford sites are small," he wrote. "The remains found at one place are usually scant." Very detailed study on some of the early findings suggest a close relationship of Piedmont Indians and western types, such as the Mohave. Relics of these earlier groups point to the fact that "they lived as isolated families and moved frequently, leaving behind scattered stone chips of their manufacture and an occasional lost or broken tool. What became of these people and their culture is unknown."

Scholars who have made a special study of the American Indian believe that some of these roaming Early

Americans reached what is now known as North Carolina about 10,000 years ago. By that time they were moving in family groups, which thought nothing of following the animals for hundreds of miles in order to find better hunting grounds. During centuries of rambling the Red Men had learned to vary their meat diet by adding wild berries, nuts, and vegetables to their food. They were beginning to enjoy the advantages of a brand new country.

INDIAN MAN AND WOMAN EATING CORN

II

THE SAURA AND KEYAUWEE TRIBES
MOVED TO PIEDMONT NORTH CAROLINA

As early as 1200 A. D. some of these wandering families had decided to live together and were beginning to settle in small villages. These settlers then built permanent houses, cleared broad fields, and enjoyed community life. Three such settlements have been positively identified has having been located about 300 years ago on the land which is known today as Piedmont North Carolina.

The exact arrival time of these human beings is not known, but records about them have enriched the pages of history. These first-known inhabitants of this area have been recorded as two separate Indian tribes, one called the Saura and the other the Keyauwee. The Saura tribe is known to have settled in two villages, Upper Saura Town and Lower Saura Town in the northern part of North Carolina; and the Keyauwee tribe built its village about 75 miles south of the Saura. The space between these settlements served as one great unfenced pastureland for wild beasts, a large wildlife area for birds and small animals, and rich farmland for village farmers and occasional dwellers outside of the settlements.

Interesting stories have been preserved about the

Indian tribes which are the first people known to have lived on the very land we walk on today. Of course the Red Men never fenced themselves in by land lines, but when the White Men took over the New World they divided the country into carefully marked sections. If Indians were known to have spent some time in one of these places, they were included in the history of that area. Therefore, even though no boundary lines were drawn around the Saura and Keyauwee while they lived in Piedmont North Carolina, when *Original* Guilford County was first created the early records of its territory included the history of these two tribes as its first settlers.

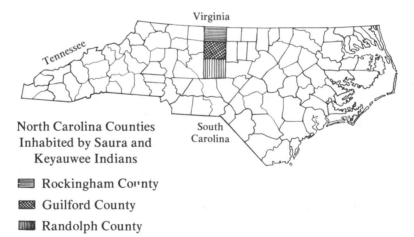

North Carolina Counties
Inhabited by Saura and
   Keyauwee Indians

▤ Rockingham County

▨ Guilford County

▥ Randolph County

Drawing by Virginia Dare Powell

NORTH CAROLINA

This map shows the large size and location of *Original* Guilford County and its later division into three parts.

III

THE LAND OF THE SAURA AND KEYAUWEE BECAME *ORIGINAL* GUILFORD COUNTY

The *Original* County of Guilford was first established over 200 years ago. At that time it was about three times bigger than it is today, and for that reason it is called *"Original* Guilford" in this story until it was divided into three parts. It was a long stretch of land which ran north to the Virginia State line and south into the heart of Piedmont North Carolina. The county courthouse was located near the center of the large division. Soon the people who lived at the most southern or most northern boundaries of this new country began to complain, because of having to go such long distances to pay their taxes, or to take care of other business matters.

Indeeed, at that time the only ways of travel were by foot, on horseback, or — a little later — by horsedrawn gigs, carriages, or stagecoaches. Therefore, the people living in the southern and northern areas of *Original* Guilford asked the State General Assembly to divide their long county into three parts, and the request was granted. The three parts were then called Guilford (1771), Randolph (1779), and Rockingham (1785).

As already mentioned, the first-known people of these three counties were the Saura and Keyauwee tribes. That was about the only positive information about them for a while, but later when Indians were more thoroughly observed it was learned that they spoke a Siouan language; that Indians were identified by the language they spoke. Whereas today we describe ourselves as having dual citizenship in North Carolina and the United States, Indians described themselves as belonging to a tribe of a certain linguistic group. According to the United States Department of the Interior, "On the basis of common words or language, there are eight major Indian linguistic groups . . . within each of these linguistic families, distinct social or cultural similarities were also present." Both individuals and tribes, which observe Indian customs, are distinguished one from another by the language which their group speaks. When historians wrote that the Saura and Keyauwee spoke a Siouan language, that meant that these were tribes of a great group which later became known as the Sioux.

In early America the Sioux was a large and powerful group. Only the Iroquois and Algonkian were larger. The Sioux was divided into two parts: the Eastern Sioux tribes, which lived in Virginia, North Carolina, and South Carolina; and the other Sioux tribes, which lived in the West.

The Western Sioux became famous in history for their victory over the white intruders and the United States army at the Battle of Little Big Horn (1876). Gold was discovered on the Western Sioux Reservation and prospectors rushed to the area, thus breaking the treaty which had provided the Reservation to the Sioux "forever." In the hope of keeping their Reservation for themselves, the Sioux, led by Chief Sitting Bull and war leader Crazy Horse, with the aid of the Cheyenne, killed the great Civil War Officer General George A. Custer and his entire force in that famous battle in Montana Territory. The Sioux is listed by the United States Department of the Interior as one of the eight great Indian groups of today.

The Saura Lived In Rockingham

The Saura Indians were first met by the European incomers in their village southeast of the present-day site of Asheville. Here the Spanish Explorer Hernando De Soto spent a number of pleasant days with them in 1540. It has been suggested by some historians that during the next 100 years the Saura had left that place and had gone farther northward to avoid trouble with still more southerly Indians, who had pushed their way into the North Carolina area in order to expand their territory. It is known that sometime before 1700 the Saura had settled in two villages — Upper Saura Town and Lower Saura Town — on the Dan River in what is now Rockingham County. When Surveyor William Byrd of Virginia was determining the Dividing Line between North Carolina and Virginia in 1728, he came across one of the Saura homesites in Rockingham County, a few miles from present-day Eden. Although

Byrd never saw the Saura, he was so impressed with the beauty of the place, which the tribe had selected for a home, that he later went back and bought a total of 26,000 acres of land in that area. In connection with his *History of the Dividing Line* Byrd wrote *A Journey to the Land of Eden* (1733), and in that account he described the land of the departed Saura: ". . . then on a sudden the scene changed, and we were surprised with an opening of large extent where the Sauro Indians once lived, who had been a considerable nation. But the frequent inroads of the Senecas [a division of the Iroquois] annoyed them incessantly and obliged them to remove from this fine situation about thirty years ago . . . . It must have been a great misfortune to them to be obliged to abandon so beautiful a dwelling, where the air is wholesome and the soil equal in fertility to any in the world. The river is about eighty yards wide, always confined within its lofty banks and rolling down its waters, as sweet as milk and as clear as crystal. There runs a charming level of more than a mile square that will bring forth like the lands of Egypt, without being overflowed once a year. There is scarce a shrub in view to intercept your prospect but grass as high as a man on horseback. Toward the woods there is a gentle ascent till your sight is intercepted by an eminence that overlooks the whole landscape. This sweet place is bounded to the east by a fine stream called Sauro Creek, which, running out of the Dan and tending westerly, makes the whole a peninsula.

"I could not quit this pleasant situation without regret but often faced about to take a parting look at it as far as I could see, and so indeed did all the rest of the company."

Although there was evidence that human beings had once lived on this land, no one was left at the place to greet Byrd and his companions. The Saura was one of the larger Indian tribes, at one time having its population recorded as 1,200 people. Its members were friendly with fourteen other large tribes and a number of smaller groups in the Carolinas.

According to Lawson, who had once visited for a few days in a number of these different villages, although there was a close bond of friendship among the tribes which shared a similar language, they spoke in different dialects. It was also noticeable that these various tribes might perform similar tasks differently, yet all of them had reached about the same level of development in their customs and mannerisms. And usually about the same degree of progress was apparent in the different linguistic groups.

It seems that the Saura was a well known tribe, for its name is mentioned in so many different spellings. The tribe name Saura was sometimes written Sauro and Souro. It was called Sara by the Catawba Indians, Suwali by the Cherokee, and Xaulla by the Spanish. Frederick W. Hodge in his *Handbook of American Indians North of Mexico* gave eleven different ways of spelling the name in one paragraph: "Charraws,

Chawraw, Saras, Saraus, Saraw, Saura, Sauro, Sawraw, Sualy, Xuala, Xualla." The name by which that tribe is now best known is Cheraw. (However, because that tribe was known as Saura as long as it remained in Rockingham County, and because local landmarks still bear that name, this story uses the name **Saura** as it was used at the time this tribe lived in the **Rockingham** area.) A number of conjectures have been listed as the possible meaning of Cheraw, but no positive definition of the name has been cited.

Indian Footprints Were Found In Guilford

In the mid-1700s when the Quakers first came to New Garden (now Guilford College), they found great open grass-covered spaces, so that very little clearing was necessary for them to prepare fields for growing their food. Some people thought that these places without trees could have been farmland where the Indians had once planted corn, or were spaces kept cleared of forests so that small wild growth could flourish for birds and small animals.

Although the Quaker minutes of 1764 stated that from the Cheraw, as they called them, the Quakers had bought and paid for the land on which they then lived, there was no mention of an Indian village in that particular place. However, some detached Indian families as country dwellers still lived in the area that became Guilford, for a few of them were seen walking around after the 1740s and 1750s when the White Men came to the region. A small number, perhaps two or three families, lived in the neighborhood of present-day Buffalo Church and were seen by the new white settlers from time to time.

It should be remembered that Indians required the use of large sections of wooded land and smaller places covered with grassy growth in order to assure good hunting. Both the Saura and the Keyauwee must have enjoyed the space which became Guilford County, because of its splendid forests and ground-covering plants which, as in Rockingham, often grew as high as a man on horseback.

The white settlers of Centre Community in southern Guilford have reported that some Indians met and befriended William Hockett, when he came alone as the first white man to establish a home in that part of Guilford County. In fact, Hockett's friends, who later joined him, said that it was because the Indians were so kind to them that their early settlement grew rapidly, whereas without such attention it might have perished. There was no known Indian village at Centre Community and it is thought that the Red Men of that place were some who had strayed away from the Catawba tribe which had a village farther south. Although the Catawba were not classed as *Original* Guilford Indians, they knew the land well; and some of their scouts helped American General Nathanael Greene draw up his plans for the very important Battle of Guilford Court House.

13

The Keyauwee Lived in Randolph

North Carolina's first Historian, John Lawson, Surveyor-General of the Province, together with five traveling companions, visited many Indian tribes of the state during 1701. It is very pleasing to learn that this journey of 1,000 miles took him to one of the *Original* Guilford tribes, the Keyauwee, which numbered about 500 people. Their village was located on Caraway Creek in the area now known as the Caraway Mountains in Randolph County, about fourteen miles south of High Point, and it gives us a good idea of Indian life at that time. Lawson's account of the visit is almost as vivid as a motion picture. He wrote that he and his company came to a village with a high wooden wall around it and large cornfields planted up to the doors of the cabins. Nearby was a great bottomland which would have easily kept 100 cows. All this was surrounded by very high mountains, so that no wind ever troubled the Keyauwee. At the top of one of the mountains there was a cave in which 100 men could have sat very comfortably to dine.

At this time, however, they had only six guests. Moreover, despite the fact that the Keyauwee had no idea that six Englishmen would appear at their village unannounced, they served the visitors their food which was already being prepared—two young deer, a country hare, venison, turkeys, and bears!

Lawson and his companions divided themselves into two parts and it was Lawson's good luck to be placed at

AN INDIAN VILLAGE

The open windows of some of the buildings furnish a glimpse of the interior benches or beds around the inside walls of the cabins.

the cabin of Keyauwee Jack, who was the Chief Ruler of the tribe. He was a Congaree Indian who had run away when he was a boy, but later became Chief because he had married the Queen of the Keyauwee. Lawson and the Chief had a good time together. When the Englishman began writing in a notebook, Chieftain Jack became very excited and wanted to try his hand at writing. Lawson wrote a word for him to copy and the Englishman reported of the Indian's first effort: "It was so well [done] that [anyone] who could read mine, might have done the same by his."

Chieftain Jack then matched his wits with his visitor by making an unusual fishhook of his own invention, and Lawson was most impressed by his host's ingenuity. Chieftain Jack was so pleased with himself at his success that he sent for several men of his tribe to look at his handiwork. While the men were all in their Chief's cabin together, Lawson took from his pocket a manual which had a picture of King David in it. Chief Jack was quick to ask who the picture represented. With this opportunity to search for the Indians' religious feelings, Lawson told him that the picture was of a good King who lived what he believed was right, "doing to all as he would be done by, ordering all his Life to the service of the Creator of all things; and being now above us all in Heaven, with God Almighty, who had rewarded him with all the delightful Pleasures imaginable in the other World, for his Obedience to Him in this." Lawson concluded with telling those present that we receive nothing here below, such as food and raiment, but what comes from that Omnipotent Being. Lawson seemed pleased that: "They listened to my Discourse with a profound Silence, assuring me that they believed what I said to be true."

Two features connected with the Keyauwee made a great impression on Lawson: the majesty and hospitality of the one Indian Princess and the whiskers of the men! He wrote: "The Queen had a Daughter by a former husband, who was the beautifulest Indian I ever saw, and had an Air of Majesty with her quite contrary to the general Carriage of the Indians. She was very kind to the English during our Abode, as well as her Father and Mother." About the fashion among Keyauwee men he added: "Most of these Indians Wear Mustachoes and Whiskers, which is rare; by reason the Indians are a People that commonly pull the Hair of their faces and other Parts, up by the Roots and suffer none to grow." *The Keyauwee were the only American Indians ever known to let hair grow on their faces.*

One might well pause for thought at this point, but with the clear understanding that it is pure conjecture. The majestic air of the Princess, the Indians' agreement with Lawson along religious lines, and the bewhiskered male faces, all of which are English traits, might suggest that the Keyauwee were connected with the Lost Colony of 1587. It had been 114 years since that group of white English settlers had disappeared; and a mixture of the races would have been possible.

After a very enjoyable visit with the Keyauwee (meaning of the name unknown), Lawson and his five companions, with one of the Keyauwee as a guide, departed for visits with neighboring tribes. On a stretch of 100 miles to travel, Lawson wrote that the only food his company had was parched corn, which he mentioned as having had for breakfast with as much ease as we speak of "Post Toasties" today.

During his 1,000-mile journey and the following seven years he was in the state, Lawson observed the habits and customs of the North Carolina Indians very carefully. For that reason his report on these first Americans is considered the most authoritative account of them. He also wrote that although each tribe had its own variations, there were certain basic rules and customs which all Indian groups followed. Because of these general ways of Indian life, through Lawson's specific descriptions of the Keyauwee and other tribes he visited, we are able to envisage the known characteristics of Indian people — their physical appearances, their homes, their food, their behavior as men, women, and children, their attitudes toward others, their fun games, their marriages, their money, medicine, religion, burials, and the remnants and memorials of those who were the first-known inhabitants of the land that later became Guilford, Randolph, and Rockingham.

IV

THE AMERICAN INDIANS WERE "PHYSICALLY FIT"

The age-old expression "straight as an Indian" had a good basis in fact, for early Indians were indeed very upright. They rarely ever slumped forward or humped in their shoulders. Their arms were well shaped and their feet and legs have been described as "the hand-somest in the world." Their skin was a soft, light brown, which appeared darker because they kept themselves greased with bear oil mixed with a color as dark as burnt cork or as red as a very ripe berry. This practice was started in infancy and continued until it filled the pores of the skin, which they thought enabled them to endure changes in the weather. Lawson wrote that the women, who painted only for special occasions, were of fairer complexion.

Their eyes were usually black, but the whites were streaked with tiny red veins, which was probably caused from eye strain. It has been said that no race had better eyes or could see better at night. This keen eyesight was a great help in locating the slightest motions made by animals when hidden in tall grass or thick woodlands.

The Indians' hair was very straight and black. Early recorders of Indian history have claimed that the Red Men were never bald; and they have stated that this was

19

the result of using bear oil and leaving their heads un-
covered. When they wished to appear particularly "well
groomed" they mixed a very special scarlet root powder
with the bear oil to give them an ornamental look. The
scarlet root, according to Lawson, also had the virtue
of killing lice and suffering none to abide or breed on
their heads.

The teeth of both Indian men and women were yellow
from smoking tobacco which they called "uppowoc."
Columbus reported that they smoked cigars. It is interesting to learn that a Spanish explorer took tobacco
plants from Mexico to Spain in the mid-sixteenth
century and that the English traders spread the use of
tobacco for smoking to others.

One feature which was especially noticeable in the
American Indians was the lack of handicapped children. There were very, very few dwarfed, blind, de-
formed, or crippled children among them. It has been
suggested by writers that this situation may have existed
because the weak and ill did not survive infancy or
because those children destined to be frail adults were
purposely allowed to perish in order to spare them later
suffering and their tribe later problems.

Another Indian feature which attracted attention was
that they prized long nails on both fingers and toes.
They contended that the nails were supposed to be
useful, the longer the better. They criticised the White
Men for cutting theirs and thus disarming themselves

INDIAN ELDER OR CHIEF AND INDIAN WOMAN

These drawings illustrate the early writers' descriptions of the "physically fit" bodies of the American Indians.

of something useful which nature had designed for them.

The White Men admired what they called the sure and stately walk of the Indians, which today we call "balance." They could walk across deep streams on small poles without any fear, or step along the ridge of a house roof to the gable end and look down to the ground, as unconcerned as if walking on the solid earth.

Artist John White, who came to what is now North Carolina with a group of Englishmen in 1585, painted splendid, descriptive pictures of Indians as he saw them in actual life. Copies of some of these drawings, scattered through this book, will give a good idea of how Indians and their way of life appeared to the first English artist in the land that is now North Carolina.

V

THE FIRST AMERICAN INHABITANTS
OF *ORIGINAL* GUILFORD BUILT HOMES

As mentioned in an earlier chapter, Red Men in general had settled into villages by the time the White Men came to America. Their major consideration for selecting a home or village site was to find a suitable place near water. Even though they knew that their first need was for nearness to water, their town sites often had the added attraction of being placed in naturally artistic settings. Of course, water made for lush foliage and other beautiful growth.

Original Guilford Indians did not live in wigwams. Lawson mentioned the private dwellings of the Keyauwee as cabins which were placed fairly close together. In building these houses they gathered very long poles of pine, cedar, hickory, or any other wood that would bend. In size these were about two or three inches in diameter. At the largest ends they generally stripped away the bark and warmed the poles thoroughly in a fire to make them tough and easy to bend. Then they placed the burned ends securely into the ground, about two yards apart, until the design they wished the cabin to be was reached. Sometimes the buildings were round, sometimes oval, sometimes rectangular. Next they bent the tops of the logs together and fastened them by using bark or moss, which was strong enough to hold them in a dome-shaped roof. Once this outline of the house was set up, the builders firmly braced it with additional poles to make the building strong.

The most tedious part of erecting an Indian cabin must have been filling in those two-yard-wide open spaces between the framework logs. Lawson wrote: "Afterwards [they] cover them all over with Bark, so that they are very warm and tight, and will keep firm against all the Weathers that blow." These dwellings were made round or circular at each end to prevent any damage by hard gales of wind. They contained an inside space in the middle of the floor for making a fire and a hole in the top of the roof directly above the fire to let out the smoke.

"These dwellings are as hot as Stoves, where the Indians sleep and sweat all Night," observed Lawson. "The Floors are never paved nor swept, so that they always have loose Earth on them. They are often troubled with a multitude of Fleas, especially near the Places where they dress their Deer-Skins, because that Hair harbours them; yet I never felt any ill, unsavory Smell in their Cabins, whereas, should we live in our Houses, as they do, we should be poisoned with our own Nastiness." At another time Lawson explained that when the Red Men were bothered with any kind of insects in home life the situation was taken care of by placing sprigs of pennyroyal about the premises, for most bugs would not stay near that wild plant.

23

Furnishings in the home were very few. There were benches which stretched all around the walls, except where the entrance door was located. On these benches were placed the skins of beasts and mats woven of various grasses, upon which people sat, slept, or lolled about. Several families of kinsmen usually lived in one house.

Outside these Indian dwellings, there were special shelters in the style of what we call summer houses, which were covered, but the sides were left open for enjoying pleasant fresh air. These had reed-hurdles like tables and were used for banquet houses during the hot season of the year. There were also houses in which grain, skins, and salable articles were stored, for in the days of the Saura and Keyauwee there was considerable trading between the White Men and *Original* Guilford Red Men.

Almost all villages had a special government house, where the Chieftain held his meetings, tribal councils, and intertribal conferences, and where special visitors from other tribes were entertained. Altogether an Indian village represented a structural social and political development that was taking place among these peoples before the White Men reached America. But specific details of such progress among the Saura and Keyauwee have not been recorded.

It is positively known that the village of the Keyauwee was surrounded by a high wall, which was made of wooden poles strongly anchored in the ground and standing as an aid in defense of the town. The Saura and Kayauwee had been frequently tormented by the Iroquois, the powerful Indian group which kept both tribes uneasy most of the time; but no assurance has been given that such a fortification would have kept a dangerous enemy from attacking the *Original* Guilford Indian homeplaces.

Sometimes first American homes were destroyed by fire. When such tragedies occurred, and all the owner's possessions were burned, the loss was not taken seriously unless the lives of kinsfolk or friends were regretted; for it was the loss of lives that always moved Indians to deep mourning, often for an extended time.

Lawson's description of a burning ceremony is very touching. He wrote that when Indian homes were destroyed by fire, the losers were ordered to prepare a feast, probably at a friend's house, and invite all of their neighbors. On the appointed day as people arrived they were served a "Mess of Victuals." Then a speaker for the occasion lamented at length about the house which had burned with all of its furnishings; and about the family which had narrowly escaped alive. He reminded those who were present that they were good friends of the homeless people, and that it was the duty of all friends to do unto the unfortunate ones as they would like to be done by. After such an oration was ended, it was customary for every man present, according to his possessions, to throw upon the ground a donation. When counted together these gifts often amounted to as much as three times the loss which had been suffered.

The same kind assistance they gave a man who wished to build a new cabin, or make a canoe. They reasoned that there are several tasks which one man cannot do by himself; and they believed that if they did not help each other their way of life would fail; then all of them would be deprived of the necessities of life.

INDIANS MAKING CANOES
Descriptions for making canoes may be found on pages 61 and 62.

VI

THE SAURA AND KEYAUWEE WERE
HEAVY EATERS AND DRINKERS

The Saura and Keyauwee were such hearty eaters as to warrent more on that subject here. They even kept food cooking in leather or stone pots day and night.

Fresh fish were abundant, for Guilford County was watered by Deep River, Haw River, North and South Buffalo Creeks, Big and Little Alamance Creeks, and (of all things!) Stinking Quarter Creek — all rising within the county. Rockingham was blessed with the beautiful Dan River and its bordering farmlands which Byrd so pleasantly described. And Randolph's Deep River and Uwharrie River just might have inspired Chief Keyauwee Jack to invent the ingenious fishhook which he so proudly showed to John Lawson.

Wild fowl populated the forests and grasslands. The story is recorded that pigeons were so plentiful that when they flew in droves they made a cloud that darkened the sky and literally broke limbs of trees when they settled to roost at night. Lawson recorded that he knew of several Indian villages which had more than 100 gallons of pigeon fat preserved for use in cooking and to spread as butter on bread. At night the Indians would go among these birds with a torchlight, kill them with long poles as they slept, and capture them by the thousands for food.

Wild turkeys, which sometimes weighed as much as 50 pounds, wandered around in great droves. Partridges and doves kept the countryside ringing with their love calls in the springtime.

And the eagle, considered the king of birds, though not valued as food, was greatly prized as an inspiration of the human spirit to develop courage and power. It was usually present on hunting expeditions, feasting on the leftovers, and stirring up conversation, for eagles were known to be different from other birds in that they breed the year round. When soft down grew on their bodies, baby eagles were left in the huge nest to keep newly added eggs warm, so that there was a continuous process of hatching. By the time the fluffy down of the first birds gave way to feathers, the second hatching had grown enough furry down to keep another set of eggs warm, and so on and on! Lawson wrote that eagles were "excellent artists" at stealing pigs, which they carried live to their nests. The pigs' loud squealing when they were being whisked through the air caused people to think they were seeing flying hogs.

Every American schoolchild should know that the bald eagle is the national emblem of the United States of America — a symbol of strength and bravery. In the days of the Saura and Keyauwee in this region, that graceful creature was known to span the sky at times without any apparent flicker of a wing, as if floating. If an eagle happened to drop one of its feathers, an Indian fortunate enough to find it cherished it as he would a rare jewel.

White Men also greatly respected the unusual bird. Once an eagle, which was shot at the site of the Battle of Guilford Court House, was mounted; and for many years, until moths destroyed its beauty, it could be seen in the Battleground Museum.

When Indians lived in *Original* Guilford, there were huge buffaloes, grazing on the wild growth as high as a man on horseback, bears which weighed as much as 300 pounds, beavers three and a half feet long, deer, the Indians' favorite meat, opossums, squirrels, and rabbits — all in such profusion that occasionally the Red Men could kill them from the doors of their own cabins.

Wild fruits and berries grew in a great variety. Strawberries, blackberries, and huckleberries were favorites on the food list of the Red Men. These they used fresh in season and dried some of them in the sunshine for use in out of season periods. These plus apples, peaches, plums, grapes, and persimmons brought a welcome relief to the dull winter diet of mostly meat and bread.

Chestnuts, acorns, walnuts, and hickory nuts held an important place in the native diet. Acorns, which were most plentiful, were widely used after they were parched and eaten as nuts or were beaten into a kind of meal and then used for thickening meat soups.

The vegetables which seemed to appeal most to the Indians were white potatoes which they called "open-

29

auk," peas, beans, squash, and pumpkins. Of course there were many more known, but as Lawson reminded, "Vegetables in Carolina are so numerous that it requires more than one Man's Age to bring the chiefest Part of them into regular Classes."

Grain was easily cultivated in the fresh soil. Wheat, barley, rye, and oats were introduced to the Indians by the Europeans, but these grains were not used as widely as Indian corn which the natives called "pagatour." This valuable food was first grown in America and next to meat provided the greatest sustenance known to the Red Men. It was planted in great fields near Indian villages and was eaten the year round. Two favorite Indian dishes were made from this native corn — loblolly, a thick mush, and rockahominy, which alone could actually sustain life for quite long periods. It was made by parching corn, pounding it into meal, and then using it in different ways in making gravy, thickening stews, or baking an Indian pudding. A handful, when moistened with water, would nourish a person for an entire day. When Indians were engaged in war or were on hunting trips the men would fasten small bags of rockahominy around their waists and serve themselves at will. Lawson commented that "The Indian Corn, or Maize, proves the most useful Grain in the World."

As may be seen, Indian food had balanced variety. One recipe which was in very high favor among them was called pemmican, and it was especially prized for its nourishing qualities. It was used to sustain hunters when they were going a great distance from home, or for warriors who had no time for hunting yet had to have food. Pemmican was a combination of dried buffalo and deer meat mixed with native fruits and berries. It may not sound appetizing to modern man, but to an Indian it was as appealing as modern man's pizza pie!

Cooking in one form or another went on from morning until evening and sometimes far into the night, for Indians ate very often, sometimes getting up at midnight to refresh themselves.

The different foods which are listed on these pages were only a very few of the edibles known to the Saura and Keyauwee. While these two Indian tribes were still living on the land that became Randolph and Rockingham Counties, John Lawson was making his 1,000-mile journey and was writing his *History of North Carolina*. In that book he used 74 pages for naming and describing the varieties of fish, animals, fowl, fruits, and vegetables available to these and other Red Men, as he had observed them firsthand. Although seeds or samples of some of them had been brought to this country by the White Men, many of them were natives of the New World.

The evolution of preparing these foods for human consumption makes an interesting story. Although there are many legends about how fire was first discovered, so far its origin has not been convincingly explained. However, the Indians first known in North

Carolina knew how to make it and use it. They had learned how to rub two sticks of different woods together with such rapid motions that the friction caused sparks to fly, just as Scouts can make fire today by rubbing two stones together. These sparks they directed into decayed wood or dry moss which burned easily. Then they would blow into the sparks until there was a flame, which they would feed with dry leaves or grass until it was able to take hold of more solid matter such as wood.

Because it was somewhat tedious to make a fire, the people were very careful to try to keep at least one small blaze alive or coals smouldering in the ashes. But, if for some reason all the fire died in a cabin, one neighbor could borrow fire from another.

It goes without saying that fire was used primarily for cooking food. At first the Indians discovered the broiling method, that is, by cooking directly in contact with fire. For a long time the New World inhabitants had no pots for boiling or baking, because their first cooking vessels were made of leather which would burn if placed directly in contact with live heat. In time, however, they learned that they could keep water hot until it cooked food by dropping hot rocks into a leather-lined pit which held both food and water. Finally they thought of shaping soapstone rocks into long cooking vessels and then they could cook directly over the fire. Eventually they made pottery or clay cooking vessels, which they hung over a roaring fire for boiling. Lawson wrote that

Courtesy of The University of North Carolina Press

COOKING FISH AND COOKING IN A POT

he had seen some pots which would hold ten gallons. Red Men needed large containers, for they cooked smaller animals and fowl whole, even with the fur and feathers still on and the insides not removed.

This method of cooking was in great fashion among the Keyauwee, and when the men of Lawson's party saw how the food was prepared, they could not eat it. It will be remembered what a great variety of meat the Keyauwee cooked at the two houses where the Englishmen

33

stayed. At one cabin they prepared two young deer and a country hare, and at the other cabin venison, turkeys, and bears. Apparently all of these were already killed and on the menu when Lawson unexpectedly arrived, for there was no mention that any Indians left the village to hunt them.

It was the custom of the Keyauwee very carefully to preserve the bones from all the flesh they ate and burn them, believing that if they failed to do so the game would leave their country and they would not be able to sustain themselves by hunting.

The Saura and Keyauwee did not have much in the way of utensils for serving food, but by 1710 they did have pottery water pitchers, from which they all drank. They also had wooden spoons, which were about the size of ladles. Old men often employed themselves by shaping pieces of wood into useful eating utensils. Even though these were placed in the pots for serving themselves, they were seldom used except for loblolly and other soups, because Indians preferred to take solid food from the cooking vessels with their hands.

It is easy to find out a great many facts about the eating habits of the Indians, but information on their drinking can be told in a short space. Granting that Red Men consumed normal amounts of water, Lawson reported one other liquid they were known to have made and drunk before the White Men arrived in America. When writing about the value of corn as a food, he added that corn stalks, which were sweet like sugar cane, when bruised and boiled made a very pleasant beer. But he gave no examples of anyone becoming intoxicated from drinking it.

Lawson, however, had many references to the Indians and alcoholic liquors which the White Men introduced to the Red Men. Thereafter many became heavy drinkers, a vice they had never known about until the Europeans came among them. Their favorite drink was rum, undiluted or "neat." Of course, all Red Men did not take it, but those who did were not satisfied to take a small amount and experience a mild reaction, but usually kept sipping until they were quite drunk. They called rum firewater and said it was a poisonous drink, yet they could not seem to keep themselves from drinking it. It was when the Indians were completely under the influence of rum that the Europeans could and often would make unfair trade bargains with them.

The Indian method for measuring this popular beverage was most unsanitary: rum was sold by the mouthful! The would-be or potential buyer would select a man who had the biggest mouth he knew of and take him to market, along with a bowl to hold the mouthfuls. The European seller would look narrowly at the great mouth, and woe to the big-mouthed Indian who swallowed during the process! According to Lawson, rum was one of the greatest enemies the Red Men had to face.

VII

INDIAN MEN WERE HUNTERS
AND WARRIORS

The Saura and Keyauwee men gave little thought to what went on at home. They felt that their role in life was to wander over the countryside in search of food. They were the providers of fish, fowl, deer, opossums, rabbits, buffaloes, and bears to feed their families and their tribes. At first they had only crude spears to aid in the capture; then they developed the bow and arrow. With the coming of the White Men, who knew how to make and use guns, the Red Men began trading furs, skins tanned into leather, pottery, hand woven mats and blankets, and a variety of trinkets for the weapons which they said "breathed fire." Indeed, they soon learned how to make guns, for Indians were quick at learning a new trade, but only occasionally did they make their own. However, the natives of the New World soon became expert gun marksmen.

Sometimes the hunters would go on long food gathering expeditions and be away from home for several moons, their way of indicating months. On rare occasions a few women might be permitted to go with the hunters, but that privilege was so contrary to the general rule that it seems almost out of place even to mention it. Some of the men were not as good hunters as others, and they were allowed to go on the expeditions to pitch camps, cook, and carry fresh meat and news back and forth to the home villages they had left behind. Indians looked upon hunting as their first responsibility, and they never grew tired of it, for, as they said, it carried pleasure as well as profit.

Sometimes it was difficult for the huntsman to locate the animals most needed for food, clothing, and shelter. In such a situation they would select a large plot of ground and set a ring of fire around it, then guide the burning undergrowth toward the center of the chosen place. As the blazing flames came nearer and nearer to the center of the ring, the animals would crowd toward that fireless spot. Thus trapped, much game could be easily captured before the fire burned out. But the frightened and distressing cries by the beasts in their helpless situation were so pathetic that the hunters lost much of their anticipated joy in their exciting maneuver.

Through countless years of hard experience, when men were at war and unable to hunt freely, these practical first-known native Americans had learned how to dry out surplus meats and in this way preserve them in times of plenty in order to have them on hand in times of want.

Although Indian men left much of the responsibility of home life to their women, they gave considerable thought to their own clothing. When first known to the Europeans, Red Men usually wore only an apron-like piece of cloth about the lower body and would never wear trousers, because such garments confined them too much and reduced their speed in running.

But they took much pride in their matchcoats, which were loose-fitting, mantle-like wraps. These garments were at times so beautifully designed that they cannot be accurately described. For warmth in winter, they were made from feathers, the skins from rabbits, raccoons, beaver, and squirrels; and for comfort in summer they were made from hand-woven materials of special wild grasses. When birds were brought home for cooking, their prettiest feathers would be saved for making fancy decorations on the matchcoats. Sometimes these coats would be made from the green part of the skin taken from the heads of mallard ducks. With threads made from the sinews of the deer or from silk grass, and needles made from the bones of deer, these thin skins were carefully sewed together. Matchcoats were especially charming when they contained a number of designs made from choice feathers which gave them the appearance of a splendidly and beautifully decorated cloak.

If garments were needed, plain wraps of this fashion were worn for everyday clothing, while the splendid types were saved for very special occasions, such as burials, dances, Thanksgiving Day festivals, or meetings with the top rulers of the tribes. It should be kept in mind that Indians, through thousands of years of experience, had developed their own forms of governments with leaders who met and made the rules by which they all lived. At these gatherings, which were great events, the lawmakers took pride in looking their best.

Their headdress must be given special mention here, because that is perhaps the best preserved and best known item of Indian dress. Almost every American schoolchild of today is familiar with the appearance of the great collection of beautiful, brightly-colored feathers, fastened to a band which fitted around the head to form a truly impressive crown.

It should also be kept in mind that the clothing of the Indian man included shoes, called moccasins, a distinctive American Indian's own design. A style still widely used to the present day, they may be finished plain or decorated with bright-colored beads. As first known, these were generally made from buckskin, but sometimes bear skin was used. Skins could be tanned into leather in an hour or two by boiling the suitable bark of trees in water and then by dropping the skins into the boiling mixture for a short time. When dried out the skins had turned into leather which would endure water and dirt without becoming stiff or hard. From this creation moccasins with no heels were made and they were a very good invention for walking, especially when men were searching near and far for food to take back to their tribes. They looked upon hunting as their most absorbing job and they took thought to make their work pleasant by making themselves comfortable.

The hair style and costumes of Indian men in peacetime were very different from those worn by them in wartime. Ordinarily, men cut part of their hair in everyday life and rolled up the long tresses, but when facing war they let their long hair down and lathered it with bear oil and red coloring. Then they added to their bodies such ornaments as feathers sticking out of their ears, rings on their fingers, bracelets along their arms, anklets around their legs, beads dangling from their necks, and any other items which would make them look different and very wild. Furthermore, many of them painted their faces red all over and drew a black circle around one eye and a white circle around the other eye. They covered their bodies with every different color of paint they could get, thus making themselves appear as hideous and horrible as possible. When these people were so smeared with paint and loaded with decorations, they were such frightful figures to look at that they appeared more like devils than human beings. The Red Men as warriors wished to be seen in disguise so that they would never be recognized, in case they were able to escape alive. And, indeed, when an Indian was in his war costume, it would have been almost impossible to figure out who he had been in peacetime.

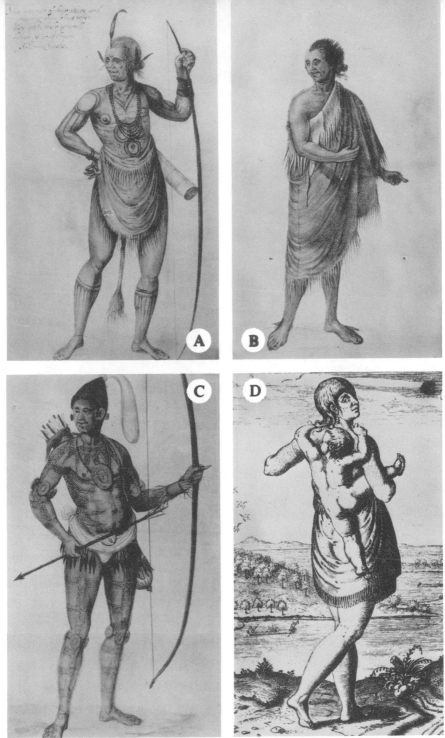

AMERICAN INDIANS IN TYPICAL NATIVE DRESS

These drawings were sketched from life by John White, the artist of the first English colony in the New World, and are used to illustrate chapters VII, VIII, and IX in this book: (A) an Indian man in body paint, "when they go to their huntings or solemn feasts;" (B) an old Indian man in a winter matchcoat (C) an Indian man in his war outfit; (D) an Indian woman and baby.

VIII

INDIAN WOMEN STAYED AT HOME

Except when traveling from one settlement to another, Indian women usually stayed close to the tribal homeplace. Only occasionally did they know the excitement of dressing up in their best costumes and using paint on their faces, or of going on long hunting journeys with their menfolk. Their role was to remain at home, do all the chores about their houses and villages, and take care of the old men, old women, and children.

This custom was generally known and accepted. Only when Indian men were building a house, making a cradle or canoe, hunting animals for food, clothing, and shelter, shaping their money, or serving in a war would they use their physical strength to get things done. A Red Man once explained to a White Man how this division of labor came to pass: "Of other work the men do none, thinking it below the dignity of their sex, but make the poor women do all the drudgery. They have a blind tradition amongst them, that work was first laid upon mankind by the fault of a female, and therefore it is but just that that sex should do the greatest part of it." It is very interesting that these primitive people had their own legend comparable to the story of Adam and Eve.

Although many of the people who have lived in Guilford, Randolph, and Rockingham Counties have been under the impression that the Indian women planted the corn in large fields which were cleared up to their very doors, Lawson wrote: "They never plant the Corn amongst us, as they do amongst the Iroquois." That is all he wrote on that subject, but he left the impression that the young men did the planting, and he later added that the men never beat their corn into meal to make bread. This task was assigned to the girls who pounded the grain with sticks, in a narrow wooden bowl, and timed their strokes so evenly together that their performance became a type of entertainment.

It goes without saying that the women were supposed to do the cooking for the family and tribal gatherings. Ned Bearskin had a word to say in this connection. Bearskin, a member of the Siouan-Saponi tribe and a close friend of the Saura, was chief hunter for William Byrd during the surveying of the Dividing Line. Bearskin told Byrd that among Indian tribes there was a strict rule that fowls and animals should never be cooked together, because that mixture was sure to bring bad luck in hunting. This must have posed a problem for the cooks, because there was only one fireplace in the house for cooking, but they did not dare disobey that ruling.

Indian women were a strong healthy group with pleasant dispositions; and no early writer about them has recorded general unhappiness in connection with their tasks. They seemed to enjoy working, and when they had free time to undertake odd jobs, they employed themselves by making baskets from bulrushes or very fine silk grass. Using these same materials they wove mats, some of which were large enough to be used for bed covers. By the early 1700s they made some cloth from cotton and flax. They were also good at making pottery, and samples of this handiwork may be seen today in museums of North Carolina. And do not forget that they made superfine matchcoats. They were very patient when doing this creative work and their garments were always neatly finished.

On one point the Europeans were disappointed in the Indian housewives, because they gave such little attention to flower gardens. Lawson remembered having seen under private cultivation only two different roses, violets, prince feathers, and two other unidentified plants. This situation, however, was understandable, because nature had been so generous in planting this country with wild flowers that it would take a sizeable volume to name them.

Women's dress had little variety. In winter it was a hairy matchcoat of a plaid design, made more for hard wear than for beauty. This was a practical outfit, for the women followed the general custom of strapping their young children onto their backs and the large garment kept both mother and baby warm. In mild weather the women wore only an apron. At first this was made from deerskin, bleached white and fringed around the bottom. If, however, they were able to trade some of their handiwork to the English for a piece of cloth, about two yards long and a half yard wide, they wrapped this around the lower part of the body from the waist to make a skirt of sorts. In time they gave tone to their appearance by making a cloth band to be worn around the waist, with a skirt gathered to it. In John White's drawings of Indian women, he pictured them in what could be called mini skirts!

Although Indian women were faithful and hard workers, they knew how to enjoy tribal dances, war celebrations, and such special occasions as Thanksgiving Day in honor of good harvests; and their springtime festival at which they sought blessings on their crops of grain, fruits, and vegetables. They never tried to surpass the dress of the men, but for these special occasions they found great pleasure in wearing fancy decorations. They pinned up their hair and used shell beads and pretty-colored feathers for their headdress. They used ornaments of bright mica or copper for earrings, bracelets, and anklets; and ropes of seashells around their necks, so long that they often fell to their waistlines. When in such costumes, they have been described as graceful and alluring. Indeed, Lawson wrote that they "have very brisk, Charming Eyes which sets them off to Advantage."

IX

INDIAN CHILDREN
WERE TAUGHT TO BE BRAVE

Indians loved their children. As soon as an Indian baby was born it was washed in cold water from the nearest stream, and then it was wrapped in moss or animal skins. The father immediately faced his first task for the infant and made it a bed. This was no big job. He took a piece of wood about two feet long and one foot wide and smoothed it into a board. He then bored holes at the top corners of the board through which straps could be arranged for holding the child safely in place. To this device the parents tied the new-born baby securely and adjusted the straps so that the mother could easily swing the bundle onto her back. The infant's back rested against the mother's back, leaving its face free to look about the world as it was carried from place to place. If it happened to rain, the mother would quickly throw her coat or shawl around herself and her child and thus would protect both of them from bad weather. This close relationship of mother and baby was usually practiced during the first year of the child's life. As a general rule, young Indians of North Carolina donned native costumes when they were about six to ten years of age.

All Indians gave names to their children, but they

were not the same as the names of their parents. They were whatever appealed to the parents at the moment. The boys kept their first names only until they were old enough to become warriors at the age of sixteen or seventeen years. At that time in life they selected their own names, which were usually chosen from nature — an animal, fish, bird, or flower—and they retained the names they selected as long as they lived. Some typical names are:

Snake Eye	Black Eagle	Rosebud
Red Wolf	Sitting Bull	Buffalo Bill
Horsecollar	Little Bear	Yellowhammer
Bearskin	Crazy Horse	Eagle Feather

Lawson noticed that Indian children were usually bright and could learn any lesson as quickly as white children. He also noticed that parents were usually kind to their children, rarely ever scolding them or making them feel inferior. If, however, they behaved badly, the elders had a quick cure for that step out-of-line. Red Men made a great use of the teeth of rattlesnakes. They pulled them from the snake, drained off any poison which might have clung to them, and then tightly fastened a few of them into a hollow stem cut from a cane stalk. With this dangerous-looking instrument a parent would scratch a place on the skin of the naughty child and require the child to watch the scratched part until it bled freely. The culprit was then forced to look at the blood until he or she felt forever convinced to stay away from wrong doing.

47

In natural interests Indian children were as responsive to their surroundings as were children of any people. Some of them have been noticed for their pet cranes which grew to almost six feet tall and became as tame as chickens. Others trained non-man-eating wolves into house dogs, for Indians had no dogs until they were brought to America by the White Men. Children loved their dogs so much that at death they buried them as carefully as if they had been human beings.

Mothers had complete care of all the young ones in a family. During this time she taught them how to do all work around the home until they were about fifteen to sixteen years of age, when the fathers took charge of the boys. Thereafter older men taught the younger men to fish, hunt, and fight. These instructions were not given until the young men had taken a very severe test. Lawson called it the most abominable custom among the Indians and he wrote about it as if it were a general practice among the tribes who had special pride in a strong race. Byrd in *A Journey to the Land of Eden* mentioned that such a training period had been practiced in Virginia. The Indians called this preparation for manhood "[Huskanawing] their young Men."

Lawson wrote that: "most commonly, once a Year, at farthest once in two Years, these People take up so many of their young Men, as they think are able to undergo it, and [Huskanaw] them, which is to make them obedient and respective to their superiors, and, (as they say) is the same to them as it is to us to send our

48

Children to School...This House of Correction is a large, strong Cabin, made on purpose for the Reception of the young Men and Boys, that have not passed this Graduation already; and it is always at Christmas that they [huskanaw] their Youth, which is by bringing them into this House and keeping them dark all the time, where they more than half starve them. Besides, they give them Pellitory Bark, and several intoxicating Plants that make them go raving mad as ever were any People in the World; and you may hear them make the most dismal and hellish Cries and Howlings that ever Human Creatures expressed; all which continues about five or six Weeks, and the little Meat they eat, is the nastiest, loathsome stuff, and mixt with all manner of Filth it is possible to get.

"After the time is expired, they are brought out of the Cabin, which never is in the Town, but always a distance off, and guarded by a [jailor] or two, who watch by Turns. Now when they first come out, they are as poor as ever any Creatures were: for you must know several die under this [strict treatment]."

Lawson expressed a desire to go to the "school" but "the King would not suffer it, because, he told me they would do me or any other white Man an Injury, that ventured amongst them, so I desisted. They play this Prank with Girls as well as Boys, and I believe it is a miserable Life they endure, because I have known several of them to run away at that time to avoid it.

"Now the [Indians] say if it was not for this, they

49

could never keep their Youth in Subjection, besides that it hardens them ever after to the Fatigues of War, Hunting, and all manner of Hardship, which their way of living exposes them to. Besides, they add, that it carries off those infirm weak Bodies, that would have been only a Burden and Disgrace to their Nation, and saves the Victuals and Cloathing for better People that would have been expended on such useless Creatures."

After telling this story Lawson seemed to have had some fear that it might make people harshly criticize the Indians for holding such a hard period of discipline. He, therefore, hastened to write that, to his way of thinking, bad as [Huskanawing] was, it was no worse than several other recorded tales of discipline practiced by White Men. And Byrd agreed with him.

This so-called schooling came at a period in life when major characteristics had already been formed, and it was a time of testing to measure spiritual and physical strength. Fortunately, the young people had been taught to have no fear of darkness, of hobgoblins, of bugbears, of fairies, of witches—all of which, as Lawson reasoned, "make such Impressions on our tender years, that at maturity, we carry Pigmies' Souls in Giants' Bodies and ever after, are thereby so much deprived of Reason, and unmaned, as never to be Master of half the Bravery Nature designed for us."

X

NORTH CAROLINA INDIANS
WERE BOTH KIND AND CRUEL

Like most Indian tribes, the Saura and Keyauwee were easygoing people in peacetime. In general, within their homes and villages, they were not quick to get mad or lose their tempers. When they had misfortunes, losses, or disappointments, they did not wear long faces or act angry. They did not try to cheat in their dealings when swapping or trading their possessions. They carefully observed their agreements about the fields on which they planted their crops, almost never taking so much as an ear of corn from a neighbor's farmland. If, however, someone did steal, he was marked as a thief and held in complete disgrace until he had paid back several times the worth of what he had taken. They never seemed to be jealous of others who were successful. They were calm in their relations within family groups and with neighbors and friends. They did not fight within their own tribes unless they were drinking or already drunk from too much rum. There was almost never heard grumbling or scolding among them. And they were free from flattery, "except Shaking of Hands and Scratching on the Shoulder", which were gestures of sincere friendship. Such kind descriptions may be found over and over in *Lawson's History of North Carolina*.

Although peaceful and undisturbed in private life, the Indians were firm to the point of cruelty when faced with the question of self-protection. Before the White Men came to America, Red Men of a given tribe sometimes fought tribes of different linguistic groups from their own, but their warfare was not carried on through great planned battles as were those in Europe. Indians usually organized in small bodies of a more dominant group and tried to destroy tribes of a different group which showed signs of growth in power. Thus they fought among themselves to prove their superior strength, valor, daring, and bravery. The victors in these small attacks punished their captives in such cruel ways that even to read about the tortures makes one shudder.

Lawson wrote that they were able to invent the most inhuman treatments for their enemies that the imagination could ever call to mind.

Here it should be clearly understood that tribes of each linguistic group, though they might be widely scattered, were loyal to that group, just as we are loyal to the United States as well as to North Carolina, wherever we are.

The Iroquois were the most warlike of the Indians known to the Saura and Keyauwee, and were greatly feared by them. These lovers of war, the Iroquois, seemed to have had a great ambition for power and they wanted to be conquerors. Indeed, according to Lawson, the Iroquois frankly confessed that they could not live without fighting. Their chief delights were war, conquest, and murder. And they did not restrict themselves to self-defense.

It might be well here to note that the League of the Iroquois, sometimes called the Five Nations, was composed of the Mohawk, Oneida, Onondaga, Cayuga, and Seneca tribes. It was the most powerful of all Indian groups north of Mexico, and its home base was centered around the Great Lakes. It extended over present-day New York State in the East to the Mississippi River in the mid-West and from the St. Lawrence River in the North to the Tennessee River in the South.

This organization was supposed to preserve the best qualities of all five tribes as they became united under a common council, each tribe being allowed a fixed number of delegates to the council. Each delegate had to be unanimously elected by his tribe and unanimously approved by the league council. There was no one person at the head of the league, and action could be taken only when approved by every delegate to the council.

The league was formed a generation before the White Men came among the Five Nations, and, according to a report from the United States Department of the Interior, it was so well regarded as a democratic plan that Benjamin Franklin is said to have been influenced by it when planning for government in the New World. It is especially interesting to note that the women had much power in the league, because lineage was based on the mother's line, and representatives to the Five Nations were nominated by the women.

Knowing that such a great force existed, it is not surprising that the Saura and Keyauwee feared any segment of the Five Nations. According to William Byrd, fighting among the Iroquois was largely by springing unexpected attacks. A small party of Iroquois men would feel a desire to conquer certain southern tribes whom they wished to weaken or destroy, would roam the country until they would locate an Indian settlement, would wait until the dead of night to announce themselves by tossing small stones into the cabins, and would then attack the sleeping party. Byrd wrote that the Iroquois had such a keen sense for locating their human objects that they could follow their tracks over woodlands covered with dry leaves. It appears that the main desire of the Iroquois was to remain the dominant group by killing members of any threatening group; and they pestered the Saura and Keyauwee because they were getting along too well to please the Iroquois.

The Indians of *Original* Guilford knew about the various punishments their men would suffer if captured by the Five Nations. Both Lawson and Byrd have written about them. If made slaves, the Iroquois and other tribes would cut the skin of their feet where the toes begin, peel it back halfway, cut off the front half of each foot and bind the skin over the incisions, so that their feet would heal as only half feet. This operation

54

made it almost impossible for the conquered one to move about fast enough to run away, or if he tried to escape he could be easily tracked. The Saura and Keyauwee were not considered as cruel in their punishment as were the Iroquois, but they also tormented their enemies when they so desired.

Another torment **practiced** on their captives by Indians in general was what they called "sculping." This operation was performed by cutting the skin along the temples and peeling off the scalp — hair and all! It was considered an honor to have scalps as proof of victorious fights.

Still another torture inflicted was by burning captives to death. The enemy, if a man of high standing such as a war captain, would be placed in a fire and forced to stay there until partially roasted. Then he would be removed for a while in order to prolong his misery, but in time was returned to his deathbed of live coals.

And still another form of prisoner punishment was inflicted by splitting pitch pine into splinters and sticking them all over the live body of the captive. After these were lighted they burned like torches, and thus dressed, the captured man was forced to dance around a great fire, while of his own accord he exhibited great bravery and endurance. Meanwhile his captors made all manner of accusations against him until he died. Then those who were present tried to get a bone from the dead body for a prized souvenir.

When these punishments were taking place, it was customary for the public to watch. Lawson was surprised to learn that the women and children took active part in the occasions by gibing and shouting accusations against the tortured one. Byrd followed his account of the punishments by citing worse crimes, to his way of thinking, which had been inflicted on their enemies by former European White Men. For example, he wrote, "Nor was Alexander the Great, with all his famed generosity, less inhuman to the brave Tyrians, two thousand of which he ordered to be crucified in cold blood for no other fault but for having defended their city most courageously against him during a siege of seven months. And what was still more brutal, he dragged —— alive at the tail of his chariot through all the streets, for defending the town with so much vigor."

It has been said that John Lawson himself died from the pine splinter torture, but Byrd wrote that Lawson's neck was slit from ear to ear. The English surveyor was going with a small group of men on an exploring trip up the Neuse River when some Tuscarora Indians, later the sixth tribe of the Five Nations, who feared that their lands might be taken from them by the White Men, captured Lawson and his party and took them before their Chief. At first the captives were released, but, according to one of the captured men, the next day Lawson got into an argument with the Tuscarora Chieftains and they sentenced him to die. Thereafter it was reported that he was burned to death.

Despite these cruel tortures which might have been used by any Indian tribe, Lawson, at the end of such descriptions, added: "The Indians are very revengeful, and never forget an Injury done, till they have received Satisfaction. Yet they are the freest from Heats and Passions (which possess the Europeans) of any I ever heard of."

BEASTS OF CAROLINA

These animals furnished food, clothing, and shelter for both the kind Indians and the cruel Indians.

Courtesy of The University of North Carolina Press

XI

RED MEN WERE LOVERS OF SPORTS

Indians were a people who admired courage and physical strength and enjoyed competitive games. In addition to their hunting and fishing, which they made part work and part play, perhaps the best known of their sport events was stickball which the Cherokee still enjoy.* Although no special attention has been called to the Saura and Keyauwee in connection with this amusement, since their nearest neighbors west of them were the Cherokee it may be assumed that the *Original* Guilford tribes had real interest in it. Indians from near and far were often present wherever stickball was in action.

The game was played between two rival teams, each of which had nine to twelve members. Only one ball was used in the contest, but each player had his own stick or bat of sorts. The stick was usually less than three feet long and resembled a tennis racket, except the end by which the ball was controlled had a flexible bowl-

* James Mooney, an authority on the American Indian, used eleven pages of print for describing the training for and performance of the play. See "The Cherokee Ball Play," by James Mooney in *Twenty-fourth Annual Report of the Bureau of American Ethnology*, Washington, 1907, pp. 575-586.

shaped network. Although the rules and ball sticks varied among different tribes, their main plays were similar.

The game was given serious attention before the players met on the ball field. Each team, directed by a special leader called a shaman, observed a period of about three weeks of various requirements and superstitions. For example, during stickball's first years of popularity, in addition to hours of practice and attentions to tribal customs, the players were placed on a diet from which rabbits and frogs were completely withdrawn. Indians agreed that rabbits were timid and easily confused and the legs of frogs were brittle and easily broken, and they feared such weaknesses might be transferred to the men who were to play.

On the night before the game, dances were held separately for each team, and the players danced around a fire all night long, pausing now and then for each man to take private and group advice from his shaman. Without having taken a morsel of food during or after the dances, on the next afternoon the two teams, led by their shamans, marched onto the center of the ball field where the game began. The field was a rectangular stretch of level ground, and at two opposite ends there were two upright poles. These were the goal posts for the two teams.

After the ball was first set in action, it was handled through the stick-bowl, without human hands touching it. However, once the ball was caught or picked up with

59

the stick-bowl, a player was allowed to take it in his hands and run toward his team's goal, until he was stopped by the opposing team. In that case the player who had the ball could toss it, if possible, to one of his party to carry forward toward his team's goal posts.

The driving action of each team was to try to be the first to pass the ball between its goal posts. This act was called a run. After each run all the players returned to the center of the field, where they began the contest for the next run. More often than not the effort to pass the ball between the goal posts became a hard-fought, sometimes violent struggle. The team which made the first twelve runs was declared the winner.

Those ingenious people also thought of other games, requiring fewer players. Lawson described these diversions as long being in use by any or all Indians. They had invented a game which was similar to a present-day game of dice. They would parch grains of corn until they were black on one side and leave the other side white, then use them as dice. Men could hardly be torn from this play, and sometimes they would play all night long. Meanwhile, through betting, they might lose their fortunes clear down to their skins, as modern gamblers (or players) do in strip poker.

Their favorite amusement, however, was played by two people. The game required only a bundle of fifty-one small split reeds, about seven inches long. These were cut and polished very smoothly so that they were easy to handle. The rules required one contestant to hold the entire bundle, quickly pull out a number of splints from the packet and throw them to his playing partner, who was to announce immediately, without counting, how many he had. Experts at this game were often able to tell as many as ten times in succession the number each player held after the throw. In this contest the motion was the quickest possible, the betting serious, and men have been known to lose in one evening everything they possessed, even their homes, and occasionally their wives.

All Indians — men, women, and children — enjoyed their contacts with water. Their homes were almost always located near streams, and swimming was their great pleasure, just for the fun of it. The Red Men had developed their own way of swimming. Unlike the White Men who used the stroke of both arms flung out at the same time, the Red Men threw their arms forward alternately, one after the other, and by that method they were able to swim faster and farther. Because swimming was open to everybody with no award prizes offered, it was especially inviting.

For both transportation and recreation, Indians used their own creation, the canoe. To make a canoe, they would take the trunk of a very large tree, spread one side with rosin or gum, which, when set on fire, would cause a hollow to be burned along the log. With stone or shell scrapers they would dig out the ashes and charcoal, then apply more rosin, gum, fire, and scraping until the vessel was completed. Such a canoe could transport as many as twenty adults. Both men and women rowed these boats for business and pleasure.*

Water furnished another important interest for the Red Men. Bathing as a part of their grooming was one of their most rigid practices. It was also a part of their religion, and was required for all, young and old, in southern climates. Even those too young, too old, or too sick to help themselves were aided to the bath waters by the able-bodied. They made quite an impressive ceremony of the occasion. Each morning, summer and winter, spring and fall, the men went first in a sort of procession, holding up their hands as if in supplication to the heavens above, then plunging forward into the water. When they had left the scene, the women then approached, singing as they marched along. Finally, giving careful thought to every member of the tribe,

---

* Indians everywhere often made valuable gifts to those whom they loved, and there is a beautiful story of the famous Chieftain, Tecumseh, who gave his English sweetheart Rebecca Galloway a canoe and took her for many happy rides in it. When he asked for permission to marry her she said she would do so only if he would give up his Indian ways and live thereafter as an Englishman. Tecumseh asked Rebecca to let him have three moons to consider her plan, then sadly he told her that he would never have any peace of mind if he was disloyal to his own people, and they parted forever. But Tecumseh, as a lasting tribute to his love, carved a wooden likeness of Rebecca in Indian dress just before he was killed in the Battle of the Thames in 1813, and that original statue is now displayed in the Greensboro Historical Museum (see page 64).

those who were helpless were carried to the water, so that they might take part in this time of worship.

Indian children were especially fond of dolls, which were made of stone, sticks, or corncobs and were clothed mostly **with imagination.** Both small girls and boys played with such toys. When boys were still very young, before their manhood training, as a sport of sorts, they learned to shoot squirrels from trees just outside the cabins, or quail strolling across the yards.

Dancing, a recreation which all Indians greatly enjoyed, and which Lawson watched on his 1,000-mile journey in North Carolina, was a sort of stamping motion. Because their dances honored different events, the Chieftain and War Captain of each tribe appointed a song writer for every scheduled dancing party, and ordered a new tune for every occasion. If war was threatened or in action, the composer made a warlike tune which expressed all the bad feelings that were known, with added thought for the punishment of any captured enemies. If all around was peaceful, his song was joyous. If dance festivals were held in the season of the year to give thanks to the Good Spirit for the fine foods and flowers of the earth, or to offer a petition for the coming harvest to be bountiful, the dance musician was instructed to make separate tunes for both celebrations, and that music was used only that one time.

All of those who were present at the dance festivals took an active part in one way or another. Sitting on a mat on the ground, two men played the dance music.

INDIANS DANCING

Native Americans celebrated almost all occasions by planning special dances and this drawing has been described as one of "Their dances which they performed at high feasts."

AN INDIAN PRINCESS

While waiting to aid the British against the Americans at the Battle of the Thames in Canada during the War of 1812, Chief Tecumseh and his band of Indians carved a wooden statue of an Indian Princess in native dress, but her figure appears to be a likeness of his English sweetheart, Rebecca Galloway (see footnote on page 62).

One rattled a gourd with beans in it and the other beat a drum which was made by fastening a deerskin very tight over the top of an earthen cooking vessel. While traveling over North Carolina, Lawson noticed that the men were wonderful dancers, and could dance for several nights in succession with the greatest alertness imaginable. "I have seen thirty odd together a dancing" and while in action they never showed any sign of being tired, but took "the most Pains at it that Men are able to endure," but when the number was over "every one dropped down with a Sweat, as if Water had been poured down their Backs."

The women could also put on a good show. Lawson was fortunate enough to see them performing, and he wrote: "This Female-Gang held their Dance for above six Hours, being all of them of a white Lather, like a running Horse, that has just come in from his Race." An added attraction was great horse bells about their legs and small hawk bells about their necks. Lawson was greatly amused that the men walked nimbly about a room without making the least noise with such bell decorations, and he left the impression that the women performed equally as well.

For these great occasions, people came from fifty to sixty miles away to attend. If they did not join in the dancing, they found pleasure in just being spectators and eating from the great pots of a favorite Indian food —loblolly—or such meats or stews as were being served, continually eating while others were dancing.

XII

INDIANS HAD SPECIAL MARRIAGE PLANS

Indians seemed to have good sense about giving attention where attention is due, and it was customary for Red Men to give much thought to marriage plans. Although unmarried young Indian men and women dated without permission, if a young man decided to settle down and make a home of his own, he would enter upon that undertaking most seriously. Having decided that he wanted a certain young woman for his wife, he (or someone for him) first secured approval of the idea from her parents or nearest relatives. Then the relatives called together all the older relatives of the prospective bride and groom and all those in the tribe, including the Chief and all his officials, and in a public meeting they openly debated the question. If the marriage idea was agreeable to the tribe in council, they, in turn, submitted the proposal for its approval by the young woman, for they never permitted a forced marriage.

Men very much preferred to have their wives already members of their own group, but when they were close relatives of the most desirable woman of their group, they were permitted to seek their brides from another Indian division. Indeed, men were never allowed to marry a woman so near related as a first cousin. And if any man secretly married his sister his body was burned and his ashes were thrown into a river.

After all these marriage rules had been observed, and consent was obtained from the proposed bride, the man then named the amount he would pay for her. That thought led to more discussion, for the prettier she was the more she was worth. The would-be groom rarely had enough wealth to pay the demanded price, but if his audience knew him to be a good hunter, and believed he could raise the demanded sum in a few moons, or in any set time they agreed upon, then he was permitted to marry the girl for whom he had asked. However, the wedding had to be postponed until he could pay the amount he had promised for her. A man was allowed to have as many wives as he was able to pay for, but usually had only one. Sometimes marriages ended in divorce, but once a couple had agreed to become man and wife, that companionship usually lasted through life.

Both Lawson and Byrd expressed the opinion that the Red Men were completely capable of becoming as good and useful citizens as the White Men, and they approved of Indians and Europeans working and living together. They felt that both races, by sharing their lives with each other, would adjust more easily and quickly to the changes taking place in the New World.

XIII

INDIAN MONEY WAS VERY INTERESTING

With the coming of the White Men, the Red Men needed money, and they designed an exchange system easily available to their own needs. It was very different from the money used by White Men. All of it was made from special kinds of seashells, which Indians carved into beads; and North Carolinians were fortunate to have the shells washed ashore on their Atlantic Coastline.

The most important of all Indian shell-money was called wampum, and it was made of dark purple, black, and white beads. The value of the beads was determined by their color, black and purple being worth twice as much as the white. Colored beads were made from hard-shelled clams and white beads from the shells of whelks (large sea snails). These shells were carved into cylinder-shaped beads about one fourth of an inch long and one eighth of an inch in diameter. They were polished as smooth as glass and were strung together by a hole drilled through the center.

Drilling was the most difficult thing to do, because the shells were very hard. Red Men were better at drilling than the White Men, probably because they had more patience. Using a very slim nail which was fastened securely in a hollow cane, an Indian would roll the cane continually on his thigh with his right hand, while he held a bit of shell in proper place with his left hand until he had drilled a hole through the shell.

The name wampum was given to the beads only when they were strung or woven together. They were made into long ropes of beads for necklaces, bound together for bracelets, and embroidered onto buckskin headbands and belts. All of these items were widely used for personal decorations. The persons wearing various collections of wampum were looked upon as successful citizens as well as being considered examples of prestige and authority.

Wampum was also used for important business purposes. For example, in trade between the Red Men and White Men, wampum was so generally used instead of ordinary coins that the White Men fixed its value by law. If wampum belts were passed from one group to another when treaties were made, they were carefully preserved in the cabins of the Indian Chiefs as historic evidence as well as public treasure. Indians claimed that these belts, when properly interpreted, could indicate the exact transaction they represented.

Indians sold their treasured money by the cubit, which in their measure meant the length from the elbow to the end of the little finger. They never thought to question the difference between a long arm of a tall man and the short arm of a small man. They had not yet learned to practice the way "to squeeze a penny!"

INDIANS FISHING

The American Indians of North Carolina fished in rivers, lakes, sounds, and the Atlantic Ocean. Fishing in the ocean was especially rewarding, for, in addition to catching a great variety of fish, along the coastline Indians were able to pick up seashells which they used for making their money.

Courtesy of The University of North Carolina Press

XIV

THE RED MEN KNEW
HELPFUL FACTS ABOUT MEDICINE

Although the Indians were unable to save themselves from the bad influence of European rum, the White Men were able to learn much from the Red Men about the treatment of illnesses. There were, and still are, a very large number of medicinal plants and herbs growing in North Carolina, particularly in its western part, such as the roots of sassafras and ginseng and the bark and leaves of witch hazel, which the Red Men introduced to the White Men. The Indians made wide use of such natural resources in the form of poultices, whereas modern manufacturers convert them into drugs. The Indians, as did all primitive peoples, figured out what plant was good for the treatment of many diseases then known among them. They thought that there was a cure for every illness in the area where it occurred.

Lawson remarked that he had witnessed too many successful Indian cures to mention all of them in his *North Carolina History*. He did, however, name a few which seemed to be never-fail-treatments for scurf, fire burns, powder burns, and ulcers.

Though their medical knowledge was truly helpful, the Indians also had their superstitions through which natives often sought help.

When simple home remedies failed to cure, they resorted to the medicine men who were always among them. Believing that all sickness was caused by the devil, these self-made doctors made themselves up so as to appear as horrible as possible, in the hope of helping to frighten away the evil spirit. Each "doctor" had his own "cures" and methods of applying them, yet some practices might be somewhat alike. Lawson has reported a number of known cases that were treated by medicine men, some of which will serve as examples.

When the frightful-looking medicine man visited the sick one, he would try to locate the pain, spurt a mouthful of warm water over it, then taking a group of rattlesnake's teeth, anchored in a split reed after the order of a comb, he would scratch the place that hurt until the blood flowed freely. Next, holding a gourd with peas in it, he would dance and caper about the sick patient until he, the doctor, was in a great sweat. His final step was to spurt another mouthful of warm water over the incision, apply a poultice of leaves or bark, and tell the patient's friends whether he would live or die.

Occasionally a medicine man was called a conjurer, who worked to get the mind of the sick man away from his pain. One time the chief man of his tribe became ill and the best-known conjurer, three days away, was summoned to treat him. Upon arrival the conjurer, who was very old and very small, asked for only two items, a bowl of water and three chunks of wood. He used the water to spurt over the patient and the wood for improvising a stool on which to stand over him. As the story goes, the doctor, standing on the stool, then held one end of a string of wampum between two fingers, while the other end touched the patient's stomach. Next he

AN INDIAN CONJURER

Indian men who practiced this art were said to be very familiar with the Bad Spirit, whom the natives thought caused all of their sicknesses or bad luck. All men of that profession fastened a small blackbird about one of their ears as a badge of their office.

Courtesy of The University of North Carolina Press

talked at length, and about a dozen witnesses thought they heard someone answering, but could see no one. At last the string of beads, hanging straight down, began to curl up and it finally rolled into a lump at the medicine man's hand. Those present were frightened until they were told that the sick man's pain would move into his leg and then he would again become well, which happened just as predicted. Lawson recorded that he had at least a dozen firsthand witnesses to this experience.

Treatment for another medical case, which Lawson included in his history, can easily be identified by anyone who has had a penicillin shot. A white North Carolina planter had an ugly ulcer on his leg and he feared that the infection might cause his death. Having tried every remedy known to him and his white physician, the planter decided to seek the advice of an Indian doctor. After looking the patient over, the medicine man mixed up a poultice, "which was nothing but the rotten, . . . Grains of Indian Corn, beaten to Powder," and applied with the soft down of a turkey. This application completely healed the ulcer. The patient lived his life out with no recurrence of the sore, and enjoyed a healthy life until he died by drowning.

One more method the medicine men often practiced to overcome illnesses was to stage a great celebration with all the excitement possible in order to make the sick forget all suffering. This "cure" was especially good for those who imagined they were ill or used sickness as a way of getting special attention.

There was also the sweat bath that was used freely. A house built for the purpose could be made so hot the bather would almost sweat himself to death in the course of the treatment, which was followed by a plunge into the coldest water at hand. If he lived to speak afterward, he could usually say in truth that he had been helped. As a matter of fact, poisons in the body can be "sweated out."

Unhappily, the White Men brought to the Red Men venereal diseases, tuberculosis, and problems related to excessive drinking of alcoholic beverages. Smallpox, an Old World disease brought to the New World, caused more deaths among the Red Men than they had ever suffered from any other illness. The Indians knew no treatment for this highly contagious sickness and they tried to cure it through the use of their well-known sweat bath. People suffering from the malady were placed in the heated bathhouse until they were dripping with sweat and then they were dashed outside and plunged into a river or a cold bath. Such treatment usually caused the death of the suffering Indian. An epidemic of smallpox within a tribe sometimes reduced the population from several hundred to less than one hundred. After the Saura and Keyauwee joined with the Catawba, that tribe became the victim of such a tragedy, and it lost about half of its population. It appears that smallpox became another of the Indians' worst enemies.

XV

THE SAURA AND KEYAUWEE
BELIEVED IN GREAT SPIRITS

The first people known to have lived in the land we walk on today were deeply religious. They thought of everything around them as a part of their daily worship. The Saura and Keyauwee Indian tribes believed that there were two Great Spirits — one good and the other bad. The good one, they said, was the maker of the fruits of the fields and the beasts and other creatures of the wilderness, so ordered that they might be helpful to man. This Great Good Spirit also made himself known through pleasant streams, towering trees, bright flowers, the sun by day, and the moon by night. They thought the winds were the messengers of this unseen God, and good winds were sent to blow His kindness upon them.

In appreciation for all these blessings, they were very careful to make their God a part of all their dances, festivals, and other public celebrations. Religion to them meant making everyday acts of their lives pleasing to the Great Good Spirit. This they did by ever remembering Him and including Him in their songs, by constantly thanking Him, and by feeling that they were always in His presence.

Courtesy of The University of North Carolina Press

INDIANS ROUND A FIRE

Native Americans enjoyed an intimate relationship with the Good Spirit and they rejoiced in their religion. This drawing has been described as "Their manner of praying with gourd rattles about a fire."

Furthermore, they believed that Red Men who lived good lives on this earth would be rewarded by the Great Spirit with all the joys that could possibly be in the next world. Such joys, however, were described as just much, much more of things they knew about — health, wealth, food, and safety from enemies — all without working for them. Lightning and thunder were proof of a power bigger than man.

On the other hand, the first inhabitants of America were quick to point out that the Bad Spirit caused people to be sick, sad, cross, and mad. Bad winds were to warn them that the Good Spirit was displeased with them because of their disregard for His wishes. Moreover, those who were lazy, cheaters, or liars in this world would be punished with sickness, poverty, hunger, and scalping by their enemies in the next world.

Both good and bad Indians feared a host of invisible spirits which they believed were around them all the time. To keep bad spirits at a distance, they carried charms for protection, repeated secret words, and always kept in their hearts a prayer for safety. According to Lawson, although the White Men asked over and over again for an explanation of their thoughts on this secret side of their religion, as a rule the Red Men would never make any reply to such questions. Their silence in connection with their private religious thinking greatly impressed their white observers.

One Sunday night that silence was broken. While William Byrd and his Dividing Line companions were sitting around their campfire they examined Ned Bear-skin on this secret Indian connection with the Great Spirit. One should not forget that Bearskin belonged to the Saponi which spoke a Siouan language, as did the Saura and Keyauwee, and Byrd reported the conversation as though Bearskin explained the secret religion that was practiced by all the Piedmont tribes which spoke a Siouan language. And he talked "without any of that reserve to which his [group] is subject."

Bearskin told the men that his people believed there was One Supreme God, that He "told the sun, the moon, and stars their business in the beginning, which they, with good-looking after, have faithfully performed ever since. That the same power that made all things at first has taken care to keep them in the same method and motion ever since."

After Bearskin had repeated the things his listeners already knew about the Indians' open religion on this earth, he told about their secret concerns for their future life after death. At that point there were only two places to go, and a big flash of lightning separated the good from the bad. The good people were directed into "a charming, warm country, where spring is everlasting and every month is May; and as the year is always in its youth, so are the people, and particularly the women are bright as stars and never scold." In this place there are animals without hunting, flowers, fruits, and vegetables without planting, and people that are never sick, never grow old, never die.

The other place where the dead might go was a dark and barren country where it is always winter, with snow the year round, and nothing to be seen on the trees but icicles. All the people are old, and have no teeth. "All the people are hungry yet have not a morsel of anything to eat except a bitter kind of potato," which makes everyone sick. In this place, sitting on a monstrous toadstool, there is a dreadful old woman whose head is covered with rattlesnakes instead of tresses, and she acts as a judge of those who enter her hell. Bearskin's further descriptions of the roads to the good place and the bad place, and other differences in after life at these places, were more than enough to make anyone wear charms and say constant prayers in order to keep the Bad Spirit at a distance.

Byrd concluded that the Indians' religious beliefs contained "the three great articles of natural religion: the belief of a god, the moral distinction betwixt good and evil, and the expectations of rewards and punishments in another world."

The religion of most of the Indians sustained them in life and comforted them in death; and they faced death very bravely. Indeed, they thought of dying as just being transferred from this earth to a better "Happy Hunting Ground."

XVI

INDIAN BURIALS WERE SOLEMN OCCASIONS

Although Indians accepted death calmly, Lawson seemed surprised at the continued attention they gave to funerals. He wrote: "Burial of their dead is performed with a great deal of Ceremony, in which one [group] differs in some few Circumstances from another, yet not so much but we may, by a general Relation, pretty nearly account for them all." From this statement one may feel assured that the Saura and Keyauwee followed the common practice, since no mention is made to the contrary.

Two facts were obvious: first, women got no great ceremony at death; and second, as a general rule, the greater the dead man had been in life, the more expensive and lengthy was his funeral. For a man, the first day and night after his death were given to mourning by his relatives. On the second day after death, burial officials went about the village in which he had lived and took blankets and matchcoats from the first young men who were wearing them, no objection occurring, and wrapped them around the dead body. To these coverings they wrapped two or three mats woven of bulrushes. And finally they made a web of woven reeds or hollow canes, which served as a coffin when it was

81

wrapped around the body several times and was tied at both ends. Lawson observed that this dressing "indeed, looks very decent and well."

When the corpse was brought out of the cabin and placed in a grave well-padded with hand-woven mats, people of the group to which he had belonged, or people of other groups in alliance with his tribe, came from near and far to take part in the ceremony. Seated around on grass mats on the ground, the people waited for the doctor or conjurer to appear. In time he came and after a long period of silence he began his oration. It took Lawson one and one-fourth printed pages in his history to list all the subjects the orator talked about. After listing all the virtues and accomplishments of the deceased, the speaker described the Country of Souls to which the dead man had gone. If he had been a fine and noble person he would have a "great Store of Deer to hunt, never meet with Hunger, Cold, or Fatigue, but everything to answer his Expectation and Desire."

When the doctor or conjurer had finished, a second speaker took over, then a third, and a fourth. Finally the lifeless body was lowered into a grave and a little roof was built over him inside the grave. If the dead man had been illustrious or great enough, in time his bones were taken out and dressed in white deerskin and mounted in a house especially built for the resting place of all their famous men who had died during the past several hundred years. No person was entitled to such splendid treatment, however, unless he had given a large sum of money to the rulers for his admittance.

Lawson added this comment: "The Women are never accompanied with these Ceremonies after Death, and to what World they allot that Sex, I never understood, unless to wait on their dead husbands."

INDIAN CHARNEL HOUSE

This drawing shows the interior of a tomb where the remains of famous tribal ancestors were kept for hundreds of years.

Courtesy of The University of North Carolina Press

XVII

DESCENDANTS OF
THE SAURA AND KEYAUWEE
MAY STILL BE ALIVE

For a long time the road to the Happy Hunting Ground for the Saura and Keyauwee seemed to have been one of deep tragedy, for what finally happened to them became a subject for speculation. Living as they did near the Great Trading Path and the Virginia Trail, which were used by the large and powerful northern tribes, such as the Iroquois, they were often attacked by raiding parties of these tormenting Indians as they roamed through the Piedmont. Being thus frequently harassed, the Saura had left their beautiful homeplaces about 1710-1711 and had united with the Keyauwee. Later both of these tribes had traveled toward eastern North Carolina with the intention of joining Indian settlements around Albemarle Sound.

This plan failed, and in the hope of finding better protection from their enemies, between 1726 and 1739 both tribes moved southward to the Pee Dee River. There they settled with or near the Catawba tribe, "which early became recognized as the most powerful of all the Siouan peoples of Carolina." By this time the Saura had been changed to Cheraw, and to this day a town by that spelling is located across the Pee Dee River from the site of their former homeplace in South Carolina. John R. Swanton, in *The Indian Tribes of North America* (1953), wrote that "They [the Cheraw and Keyauwee by those names] do not reappear in any of the historical records but probably united ultimately in part with the Catawba, while some of their descendants are represented among the Robeson County Indians" of North Carolina.

A later thought on the Saura-Cheraw has come from Stanley A. South in his *Indians in North Carolina* (1972). In this book he states that by 1750 the Cheraw had left their homes near the present-day town of Cheraw and part of them had moved in with the Catawba. One section of them, however, refused to unite with the Catawba and those Saura-Cheraw may have gone into what is now Robeson County, North Carolina, where the Lumbee Indians are now living. Indeed, the Lumbee Indians may possibly be descended from the Saura-Cheraw who so bravely risked their lives to maintain their independence.

So far as is now known, most of the Keyauwee joined the Catawba tribe when some of the Saura made that move. Many years later some of the Catawba, including parts of the Saura and Keyauwee, joined the Cherokee in North Carolina, but sometime later most of them returned to South Carolina where they still live. However, while they were in North Carolina, some of the Saura-Keyauwee-Catawba intermarried with the Cherokee, and, according to Swanton (1953), still live there. Meanwhile a few others went to the area of the Cherokee

THE ARRIVAL OF THE ENGLISH

Roanoke Island and vicinity, where Sir Walter Raleigh's First English Colony of White Men met American Red Men. Here the English built Fort Raleigh and "decent dwelling houses," as may be seen in John White's drawing.

Nation in what is now Oklahoma, and from there scattered into Oklahoma. Although these have been reported as extinct, others have been recorded as having moved into Arkansas and Colorado, where they have been gradually absorbed by western Red Men and White Men. It could be that blood of the Saura-Keyauwee-Catawba-Cherokee combination may be mixed with blood of the White Men from the South to the West of the United States.

XVIII

RED MEN MADE THE WORLD BETTER

As if leaving their own memorials, the Saura and Keyauwee sowed the earth with their relics, such as tomahawks, crude plows, hand-carved pipes. pottery, decorative and trade beads, and arrowheads, many of which have been picked up in *Original* Guilford county. Today samples of these may be seen in the Greensboro Historical Museum. In special honor of the Keyauwee we have the Uwharrie Mountains, Uwharrie River, and Caraway Mountains and Caraway Creek. And we have abiding memories of the Saura in Saura Town, Saura Mountain, Sewali Gap, and the Town of Cheraw in South Carolina.

In general, however, traditions and benefits which the White Men have gathered from the Red Men have not been taken from any particular tribe, but from the Indian race as a whole. In mentioning some of the Indian ways and customs which still live with us, we must remember that the Saura and Keyauwee were a respected part of the Indian race which made these definite living contributions.

Some of our more general national practices which can be attributed to the Indian race as a whole, of which the Saura and Keyauwee were worthy tribes, have been highly valuable in the development of American life. The Indians taught the White Men how to make medicines from certain local herbs and plants; how to grow and use tobacco, white potatoes, and Indian corn. They made the Great Trading Path, the Virginia Trail, and numerous other passageways which have become roadbeds for modern highways and railroads. Although at first they could not read and write, they could and did draw maps which were very helpful guides to many settlements in the New World. The Indians left traditions which have served as basic rules for the worthy organizations of the Girl Scouts and Boy Scouts of America. Although there had been traditional days of thanksgiving to the Gods of all men since the beginning of time, the American Indians' impressive Thanksgiving Day, showing appreciation to their Great Spirit for the bounteous harvests, inspired the White Men to unite with Chief Massasoit and his Indians at a great fall festival with the Plymouth Colony in November, 1621; and that occasion eventually inspired the idea for our National Thanksgiving Day.

Although we do not see many Indians in person as we travel in the United States today, yet we do not go many miles before we see Indian names, for they are implanted all over the country. Indeed, half of the United States were named for Indian tribes or people:

Alabama	Arizona	Connecticut
Alaska	Arkansas	Illinois

Iowa	Mississippi	Oklahoma
Kansas	Missouri	Tennessee
Kentucky	Nebraska	Texas
Massachusetts	New Mexico	Utah
Michigan	North & South Dakota	Wisconsin
Minnesota	Ohio	Wyoming

Furthermore, practically every state in the Union has cities or other subdivisions with Indian names.

Ten of the largest rivers in our country and many of the smaller streams have been named for Indians:

Alabama River	Mississippi River
Apalachi River	Missouri River
Arkansas River	Ohio River
Catawba River	Susquehanna River
Chattahoochee River	Tennessee River

And four of the Great Lakes honor Indians with their names: Erie, Huron, Michigan, and Ontario.

Minor American Poet Lydia H. Sigourney (1791-1865) was impressed with the enduring records Indians have implanted in this country. In her poem "Indian Names" she wrote:

> But their name is on your waters
> Ye may not wash it out.

REFERENCES

Hodge, Frederick Webb, ed. *Handbook of American Indians North of Mexico*. Washington, Government Printing Office, 1912.

Lawson, John. *Lawson's History of North Carolina*, edited by Frances Latham Harriss. Richmond, Garrett & Massie, Inc., 1952.

Mooney, James. "The Cherokee Ball Play," *American Anthropologist*, cited in *The American Indian in North Carolina*, by Douglas L. Rights, Durham, Duke University Press, 1947.

——————, and Swanton, John R. "The Aboriginal Population of America North of Mexico," *Smithsonian Miscellaneous Collections*, VIII, No. 7. Washington, 1928.

Rights, Douglas L. *The American Indian in North Carolina*. Durham, Duke University Press, 1947.

South, Stanley A. *Indians in North Carolina*. Raleigh, State Department of Archives and History, 1972.

Stoutenburgh, John L., Jr. *Dictionary of the American Indian*. New York, Philosophical Library, Inc., 1960.

Swanton, John R. *The Indian Tribes of North America*. Washington, Government Printing Office, 1953.

United States Department of the Interior, Bureau of Indian Affairs. "Answers to Your Questions about American Indians," "Indians of the Eastern Seaboard," "Indians of the Gulf Coast," "INDIANS: Surviving Groups in Eastern and Southern States."

White, John. *The American Drawings of John White*, edited by Paul Hulton & David Beers Quinn, Volumes I and II. London, The Trustees of the British Museum, Chapel Hill, North Carolina, The University of North Carolina Press, MCMLXIV.

Wright, Louis B., ed. *The Prose Works of William Byrd of Westover*, including "History of the Dividing Line," "A Journey to the Land of Eden," etc. Cambridge, The Belknap Press of Harvard University Press, 1966.

INDEX

91

INDEX

Keyauwee Jack, 16; fishhook, 16, 27
Keyauwee village described, 14; tribal size, 14

Lakes named for Indians, 89
Lawson, John, 1; visits Keyauwee, 14, and is quoted throughout this book as a primary source on Indians and their way of life in the early 1700s
Little Big Horn, Battle of, 8-9
Loblolly, 30
Lower Saura Town, 5, 9, 87

Marriage, 66-67
Massasoit, Chief, 88
Matchcoats, 38; and moccasins, 39
Money, 68-70
Mongoloid, 2
Mooney, James, 58n
Medicine men, 72-75
Men at home, 36, 42; at hunting, 36-37; at dressing, 37-39; at warring, 40

Names of Indians, 47
New World, 1, 2, 3, name given to what is now the land of the Americas and their possessions, and is so used throughout this book

Original Guilford County, 1, 6, 7, a name used in this book for the County before it was divided into three parts, and is used throughout the book when referring to its earliest history.
"Openauk," 29-30

"Pagatour," 30
Pemmican, 30, 31
Penicillin, 74
"Physically Fit", 19-21
Piedmont North Carolina, 5, a division of land in the central part of the state
Pigeons, 27
Plymouth Colony, 88
Potatoes, white, 29, 88
Princess of Keyauwee, 17

Quakers, 12

Randolph County, 7, 18, passim

Recreations, 60-63
Red Men, 1, 4, 6, a name used interchangeably with Indians throughout this book
Religion's three great articles, 80
Rivers named for Indians, 89
Rockahominy, 30
Rockingham County, 7, 18, passim
Rocky Mountains, 2
Rum, 35, 71

Saponi, 43, 79
Sassafras, 71
Saura, 5, 6, 7, 8, 9, 10, 11, thereafter mentioned throughout this book
Saura Mountain, 87
Saura Town, 87
Senecas, 10
Sewali Gap, 87
Siberia, 1
Sioux Indians, 8
Smallpox, 75
South, Stanley A., 85
Sports, 58
States named for Indians, 88-89
Stickball, 58-60
Swanton, John R., 85
Sweat bath, 75

Tecumseh, Chief, 62n, 64
Thanksgiving Day, 88
Tobacco, 20, 88
Tuscarora Indians, 56

Upper Saura Town, 5, 9
"Uppowoc," 20
U. S. Dept. of the Interior, 8, 9, 53
Uwharrie Mountains and River, 87

Vegetables, 29-30
Virginia Trail, 84, 88

Wampum, 68-70
Women and work, 42-44; dress, 44-45; pleasure, 45; politics, 53-54; burial, 83
White, John, 21
White Men, 6, 12, a name used interchangeably with Europeans throughout this book
Witch hazel, 71